BY SAM AND BERYL EPSTEIN

ILLUSTRATED BY VICTOR MAYS

D1709979

GARRARD PUBLISHING COMPANY
CHAMPAIGN, ILLINOIS

1658

920
E
c. 1
(4-6)

Sports Consultant:
COLONEL RED REEDER
Former Member of the West Point Coaching Staff
and Special Assistant to the West Point
Director of Athletics

Library of Congress Cataloging in Publication Data

Epstein, Samuel, 1909–
  More stories of baseball champions.

  (Sports library)
  SUMMARY: Traces the careers of three baseball
stars elected to the Baseball Hall of Fame in 1937.

    1. Young, Denton True, 1867–1955—Juvenile
literature. 2. Lajoie, Napoleon, 1875–1959—Juvenile
literature. 3. Speaker, Tris—Juvenile literature.
4. Baseball—Biography—Juvenile literature.
5. Cooperstown, N. Y. National Baseball Hall of
Fame and Museum—Juvenile literature. [1. Young,
Denton True, 1867–1955. 2. Lajoie, Napoleon, 1875–
1959. 3. Speaker, Tris. 4. Baseball—Biography]
I. Epstein, Beryl (Williams) 1910–   joint author.
II. Mays, Victor, 1927   illus. III. Title.
GV865.A1E59   796.357′092′2 [920]   73-2941
ISBN 0–8116–6664–6

Photo credits:

Boston Public Library, Print Department: p. 27 (both)
Brown Brothers: pp. 6, 29, 36, 59 (top), 66, 88, 95 (top)
Culver Pictures: pp. 17 (both), 32, 50, 72, 81, 91
National Baseball Hall of Fame: p. 4
Photoworld: p. 59 (bottom)
United Press International: pp. 8, 62
Wide World: p. 95 (bottom)

Contents

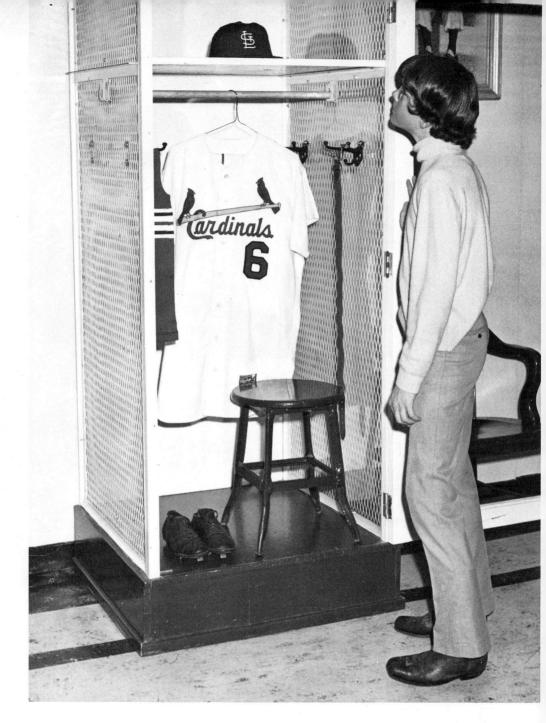

Days of glory live again for a young fan in the Baseball Hall of Fame.

Hall of Fame Heroes

Thousands of baseball fans visit the Baseball Hall of Fame at Cooperstown, N. Y., every year. There, they can see the bronze plaques honoring the game's greatest stars. There, they can see souvenirs of their favorites.

Three of those souvenirs are a ball, a glove, and a uniform. Each belonged to one of baseball's great early heroes.

The ball was slammed by the handsome slugger, Napoleon Lajoie, for his 3,000th hit.

In the early 1900s fans crowded the stands
and spilled onto the field to see Cy Young,
Nap Lajoie, and Tris Speaker play ball.

The glove was used by that amazing
pitcher, Denton T. Young. Young won more
major-league games than any other hurler
who ever lived.

The uniform was worn by Tris Speaker,
often called the greatest defensive center
fielder in the history of baseball.

Those three men were elected to the Hall
of Fame in 1937, one year after it was

founded. Baseball fans everywhere said no one deserved the honor more than they did. (The first five men, elected in 1936, were Ty Cobb, Honus Wagner, Christy Mathewson, Babe Ruth, and Walter Johnson.)

At one time the names of Speaker, Young, and Lajoie were known from coast to coast. Today some people have forgotten these three players. But to every real baseball fan, they are still as famous as they were when crowds cheered them from the stands. This book tells you their stories.

Denton T. Young
The Canton Cyclone

One day in the spring of 1890, a young man walked up to the edge of a ball field in Canton, Ohio. He watched the Canton team practice. Then he called out, "Where can I find Mr. Moreland, your manager?"

The players looked at him. "A hayseed right off the farm!" one said.

The young man was big—so big that his clothes didn't fit him. His pants were too short. His sleeves were also too short. His hat perched high on his head. A cheap cardboard suitcase hung from one of his huge hands.

"I'm Moreland," a man said. "Who are you?"

"Denton T. Young, Mr. Moreland," the young man said. "I live in Gilmore, about fifty miles south of here. I'm a farmer," he added.

"I could have guessed that," George Moreland said. He was trying hard not to smile. "What can I do for you?" he asked.

"I'd like to try out for your team," Denton Young said. "I'm a pitcher."

"Well! I never would have guessed that!" Moreland said. "Where have you played?"

"On semi-pro teams around Gilmore," Young told him. "And out in Nebraska where I lived for a while."

"All right," Moreland said. "Let's see what you've got." He ordered his best batter to the plate.

"Now we'll have some fun," the batter told his teammates.

Denton Young put down his suitcase. He took off his hat and jacket and laid them on top of it. He rolled up his sleeves. Then he picked up the ball and walked out to the mound.

"Heave it, farmboy!" the batter called.

Young's arm whipped forward. The ball whistled across the plate and crashed into the little wooden grandstand behind it. A board split under the blow.

There was a surprised look on the batter's face. "Try it again," he said grimly.

Someone trotted after the ball and threw it back to the mound.

Once more Young threw. Once more it was a sizzler. The batter swung at the ball —and missed. Once more it crashed into the grandstand, and another board was split.

Young threw six more pitches. Each time his ball whistled past the amazed batter. Each time the grandstand suffered.

12

"That's enough!" Moreland said then. "The grandstand can't take anymore. It looks as if a cyclone had struck it." He walked up to the pitcher's box. "You're on the team," he told Young. "I've even got a good name for you. We'll call you Cy, short for cyclone."

Cy Young was twenty-three years old when he joined the Canton team. He was 6 feet 2 inches tall and weighed 210 pounds.

Long hours of work on his father's farm had made his body tough and hard. Sawing wood and splitting rails had given him a powerful right arm. From early boyhood he had used that arm throwing stones at trees. He had begun to play baseball as soon as he could hold a bat.

Cy Young pitched his first game for Canton on April 30, 1890, against a team from Wheeling, West Virginia. He struck out six men. He walked one. He allowed the

Wheeling team only three hits. Canton won, 4–2.

Cy pitched thirty more games for Canton during the next three months. On July 25 he went to the mound for his thirty-first game. Canton was playing a team from McKeesport, Pennsylvania.

The McKeesport batters seemed helpless against his sizzling ball. Cy struck out eighteen of them and walked none. McKeesport got a single run only because of Canton's errors in the ninth inning. Canton won, 4–1. Cy Young had pitched a no-hit game!

News of that game reached the manager of the Spiders, the National League team in Cleveland. "We could use a pitcher like that," Pat Tebeau said.

Tebeau bought Cy Young for $250. A few days later, on August 6, he decided to let his new man pitch against the Chicago White Stockings.

Tebeau knew he was taking a big chance with his young rookie.

"Cap Anson is one of the best sluggers in the league," he told Cy.

"I know," Cy said.

Everyone had heard of Adrian Anson, the Chicago captain. Many experts thought he was the finest batter of his time.

"I'm going to have to pitch to Anson someday," Cy said. "It might just as well be today."

"Hey there, hayseed!" the Chicago players yelled at Cy as he walked to the box.

Cy looked as if he had not heard them.

He struck out the first Chicago batter. He struck out the second. Then Cap Anson came up to bat.

"Get the straw out of your hair, hick!" Anson jeered.

"Let the farmboy alone!" some of the fans shouted. "He's doing all right!"

Cy's first pitch to Anson whistled across the plate past Anson's shoulder.

"Strike!" the umpire yelled. The fans cheered.

Anson glared at the fans and then at Cy.

Cy's second pitch was another screamer that cut cleanly across the plate.

"Strike two!"

When Cy's next ball streaked for the plate, Anson swung with all his might. But the ball broke sharply just before it reached him.

"Strike three!"

A chorus of jeers from the fans and the Cleveland Spiders followed Anson as he went back to the bench.

That was just the beginning. While the Spiders piled up eight runs, the White Stockings earned only one. Cy Young held them to three hits—and Cap Anson did not make one of them!

Cleveland's Cy Young (above) demonstrates the pitching style that shut out Cap Anson (right), Chicago's star slugger.

Cy soon became a favorite with the Cleveland fans.

The next year was Cy's first full season in major-league ball. He won twenty-seven games and lost twenty. For the next thirteen years he would go on winning twenty or more games each season. And in five of those seasons, he would win more than thirty games. In 1892 he won thirty-six. In 1893 he won thirty-two.

Baseball was a rough game in those days, and the Spiders were one of the roughest teams in the league. Tebeau and most of his players didn't even mind knocking a runner down if they thought the umpire wasn't looking.

Cy Young didn't join in that kind of rough play. He could protect himself against opposing players if necessary. But he didn't start trouble. During a game he thought about only one thing—his pitching.

Cy's favorite pitch was the straight fast ball that sizzled across the plate just below the batter's chin. He had another pitch that dropped sharply downward. And he had a good wide-breaking sidearm curve. But his best weapon against batters was his control. Cy could put a ball just about where he wanted it to go.

Another important weapon was his great strength. He could pitch every third day without getting tired.

"How do you do it, Cy?" his fans asked.

"It's easy if you're a farmer," he always told them.

Cy had bought his own farm as soon as he knew he was going to earn a steady salary as a ballplayer. It was in the little Ohio town of Peoli. After he married his childhood sweetheart, they spent every winter there. Cy enjoyed all the farm chores.

"Sawing and splitting wood keeps my

throwing arm in condition," he told his fans. "Hunting keeps my leg muscles tough and limber. Why, I can pitch after only one day of rest if I have to."

In 1895 Cy Young won thirty-five victories and the title of the National League's leading pitcher. Since there was only one league in those days, this meant he was the best pitcher in the country. This was the first of the three years he would win that honor.

That same year the Cleveland Spiders and the Baltimore Orioles agreed to play a seven-game series after the regular season. The winner would be awarded a cup and the title of league champion.

This kind of a series was a new idea at the time. The fans were enthusiastic. They knew the games would be fought hard.

The first three games were played in Cleveland. Cy Young pitched two of them. Cleveland won all three.

Then the teams moved to Baltimore. The Baltimore fans were wild. They wanted revenge. They hurled bottles and insults at the visitors. Police had to be called to protect the Cleveland players.

Baltimore won the fourth game and kept the series alive.

The next day the Baltimore fans were in an even greater uproar than before. When Cy went out to the pitcher's box, they jumped up and down. They yelled and screamed. They did everything they could think of to upset the pitcher who had already beaten the Orioles twice.

Cy kept calm. Steadily, as if he were chopping down a tree, he hurled pitch after pitch. And he hit a two-bagger that helped Cleveland to a 5–2 victory.

The series was over. The Spiders were the baseball champions of the nation, and Cy Young was their star.

The year 1897 was an especially exciting one for Cy's fans. In a game against Cincinnati, he led his team to a 6–0 victory. He had walked one man, but he had not yielded a single hit. He had pitched another no-hit game, this time in the major league.

Two years later the owner of the Spiders bought the St. Louis Cardinals. He sent some of his best Cleveland players to his new team, to strengthen it. Cy Young was one of them.

On the afternoon Cy was to pitch his first Cardinal game, there was a trolley strike. Cy thought he would play to empty stands, for most St. Louis fans then went to the ball park by trolley. But the fans were determined to see their new star. They rode out to the field in wagons and buggies, on horses and bicycles. Many of them walked. By game time over 10,000 of them had jammed the stands.

Cy didn't disappoint them. He led the Cardinals to an 8–0 victory.

That first year with the Cardinals he won twenty-six games. He won twenty the next year. But he couldn't feel at home in St. Louis.

He was ready to think of moving when the new American League was organized. Its owners were doing their best to hire some of the best National League players. The owner of the new Boston Red Sox team offered Cy $3,000 a year. That was $600 more than Cy was earning with the Cardinals.

The Cardinals' owner didn't try to hold him. "Young is thirty-three years old," he told his friends. "He's getting fat. He might last a while in that new bush league. But he won't be able to stand the pace in the National League any longer."

So in 1901 Cy Young went to Boston. His first year there proved how wrong the

Cardinal owner was. Cy pitched forty-three games and won thirty-three of them! He stood the pace as well as any twenty-year-old. His famous control was as good as ever.

In 1902 Cy won thirty-two games against twelve losses. That was his fifth and last thirty-plus season. But he didn't drop very far the next year. In 1903 he helped Boston win the American League championship by winning twenty-eight games and losing ten.

That was the year the National League challenged the new American League to a post-season series of nine games. It was not called a World Series, but it set the pattern for those contests. It pitted the Boston Red Sox against the National League champions, the Pittsburgh Pirates.

The whole country kept score on that series. The first team to win five games would win the contest.

Pittsburgh took the first game, beating pitcher Cy Young 7–3.

Boston won the second game. But it lost the next two. It was now well behind in the series, one game to three.

Then Cy won the fifth game for Boston, with a score of 11–2. And Boston won the sixth game, tying the series score 3–3.

Again Cy went to the pitcher's box for the seventh game. He won it 7–3, to put Boston one game ahead. When Boston won the eighth game, 3–0, the Red Sox took the series and the title of national champions.

Cy Young was now as much a hero in Boston as he had been in Cleveland and St. Louis. He was thirty-six years old. But he had pitched three of the series games and won two of them!

The next year he played a game his fans would never forget. The Red Sox were facing the Philadephia Athletics. The

In the 1903 series: scrappy Cy Young (above) jumps up to dispute a decision, while his teammates tangle with the law.

Philadelphia pitcher was Rube Waddell, a left-hander, one of the great pitchers in baseball history.

Cy's fans packed the Boston stands that day. Some of them worried about the tough competition their aging hero was about to meet.

In the first inning, three Athletic batters came up and three went down.

Inning after inning the same thing happened.

The best any Philadelphia player could do was to bat an easy grounder or a pop fly.

Cy struck out eight men. He walked no one. Not a man on the Philadelphia team reached first base. Cy Young had pitched one more no-hitter, and this one was a perfect game!

Fans were not the only ones who loved Cy Young. He was a favorite with his teammates too. Once they gave him a birthday

Philadelphia pitcher Rube Waddell was the victim of Cy's brilliant no-hit game.

party and presented him with a cup. On it they had engraved DENTON TECUMSEH YOUNG.

Cy started to tell them that they had made a mistake. His middle name was not Tecumseh, but True. Instead, he just thanked them and told them how pleased and proud they had made him.

"I didn't want to hurt their feelings," he told a sportswriter later. "They had gone to a lot of trouble to be nice to me."

"But where did they get the idea that your middle name was Tecumseh?" the writer asked.

Cy grinned. "Some sportswriters used to call me the chief of the pitchers," he said. "So I guess my friends figured that T stood for Tecumseh, the name of a great Indian chief."

The Indian name stuck to Cy. It even appears on some of his records in the Baseball Hall of Fame.

In 1905 Cy won only eighteen games and lost nineteen. The next year was even worse. He won thirteen and lost twenty-one.

His fans wished he would retire. "Why doesn't he quit before he spoils his terrific record?" they wondered.

But Cy said stubbornly, "My arm feels as good as ever. I'll keep on until it goes bad."

Then in 1907 his losses dropped to fifteen, and he won twenty-two games! And in 1908 he won twenty-one and lost only eleven! That same year he pitched his third major-league no-hitter, against the New York Highlanders. The team was later called the Yankees.

The Boston fans wanted to honor their forty-two-year-old pitcher. They planned a Cy Young Day at their ball park.

Twenty thousand people crowded into the stands for the celebration. Another 10,000 had to be turned away. Everyone cheered the guest of honor. Many of them had brought him presents. One gift came from his fellow players in the American League. Another came from the league's umpires. The fans themselves had collected $7,500 for their favorite Red Sox. That was more money than Cy earned in a year of playing ball.

Once more, at the end of that season, the owner of Cy's team decided Cy was too old

Sold to the Cleveland Indians, the aging Cy Young warms up before a game.

for the game. The Red Sox sold Cy to the Cleveland Indians. The Boston fans were shocked.

Cy said only, "Well, it will be good to be near my farm again. I'm always happiest when I'm in the Ohio countryside."

He gave Cleveland one fine season, piling up nineteen wins against fifteen losses. The next year his score fell to seven wins and ten losses. In the middle of the following

32

season, in August 1911, Cleveland dropped him from the team.

Cy finished out that year with the Braves of Boston. His old friends in that city turned out to see him every time he played. He appeared for training with the Braves the next spring. But before the season started, he knew his arm was failing him.

"I guess I'll have to call it quits," he told the manager. He was forty-six years old.

The people of Peoli were glad to have Cy Young at home all year round. They became angry when the United States government said the Peoli post office would be closed. Peoli was too small to have a post office of its own, the government said.

"The government can't do that!" Cy's neighbors said. "Cy Young lives here! And he gets a lot of fan mail from all over the country!"

An Ohio congressman took their message

to Washington. The government changed its mind. The Peoli post office stayed open, and mail went on pouring into it for Cy Young.

After his wife died in 1933, Cy felt lonely on the farm. He had no children to share it with him. Soon he moved to nearby Newcomerstown.

On March 29, 1947, the little town of Newcomerstown gave Cy a huge party on his 80th birthday. Over 750 people came to celebrate the day with him.

Eight years later, on November 4, 1955, Cy Young died.

He had set many records during his twenty-two years in the major leagues. Once, for example, he had pitched twenty-three innings in a row without allowing a single hit. Another time he had pitched twenty innings without walking a batter. He had pitched three no-hitters, one of them a perfect game.

Since his death some of his records have been broken. But most sportswriters agree that no pitcher will ever break one of them: Cy played 906 games in the major leagues and won 511 of them.

Once, when Cy was an old man, a very young sportswriter joined the crowd around him during a Cleveland game. The young man didn't know who Cy was.

"Pardon me," the writer said, "but were you a pitcher?"

Cy smiled. "Son," he said, "I pitched—and won—more games than you're likely to see in your lifetime."

The other writers in the crowd grinned and applauded. They knew Cy was right.

In 1957 organized baseball set up an annual award for the most valuable pitcher in each league. In honor of one of the greatest pitchers in the game's history, they named it the Cy Young Award.

Napoleon Lajoie
The Big Frenchman

The pitcher of the New York Highlanders was worried. Cleveland had two men on base. The next Clevelander coming up to bat was Napoleon Lajoie, the man most people called Nap, or Larry.

Nap was over six feet tall. His hair was jet black. He moved with the smooth grace of a cat. His heavy bat hung from his hand as if it weighed nothing at all.

The Highland catcher signaled the pitcher. "Walk him," the signal said.

The pitcher's first throw was far from the plate. Nap didn't even try to reach for it.

"Ball one!" the umpire called.

The next pitch was again far outside. "Ball two!" the umpire said. After the third wide pitch he said, "Ball three!"

Nap Lajoie shifted his grip on the bat. Now his hands were close together at the very end of the stick.

Once more the pitcher hurled the ball. The catcher stretched far to the right, ready for another outside one.

Nap's left hand dropped from his bat. His right arm reached far out, with the bat at the end of it. One-handed he swung!

Crack! The wood connected for a solid hit!

Both of Nap's teammates raced home to score while he trotted easily to second.

Twice more during that game the Highland pitcher tried to walk Nap Lajoie. Each time Nap slammed the ball one-handed. Each time he got a two-base hit.

Finally the pitcher walked him by throwing four balls behind the Cleveland slugger. "Even Nap Lajoie," a baseball reporter wrote, "couldn't hit a ball with his backside."

Napoleon Lajoie was born September 5, 1875, in Woonsocket, Rhode Island. His French-Canadian parents were poor. When Napoleon was five years old, his father died. Then the family was poorer than ever.

Napoleon and his brothers and sisters went to work as soon as anyone would hire them. At first Nap did odd jobs after school. When he finished the eighth grade, he left school to take a regular job in a lumberyard.

Somehow he also found a few hours each week for a game of baseball. It was the one thing that brought real joy into his hard life. He played during his lunch hour, after work, or on Sundays.

Most of the boys he played with were as poor as he was. Their ball was usually ragged and so old that it was almost black with dirt. But they played a good game, and Napoleon Lajoie played best of all.

Soon the older ballplayers in Woonsocket began to talk about him.

"Have you seen that French kid with the funny name?" a young man asked his teammate one day.

"I sure have," the teammate said. "He can really clout a ball! He told me the right way to say his last name is Laj-o-way."

"Both his names are too much for me," the first man said. "I just call him Sandy. He doesn't mind. He's got a reach like a giraffe!" he went on. "And he probably isn't even fifteen years old!"

"We could use that kid," his teammate said. "Let's ask him to play with us next Sunday."

40

So Napoleon Lajoie began to play with some of the regular grown-up teams around Woonsocket.

At the end of one Sunday game, a man stopped him as he was leaving the field. "I've been watching you," he said. "How would you like to play with our team, the Globe Stars?"

Napoleon was surprised. "That's a pro team, isn't it?" he said.

"Semi-pro," the man said. "The players pick up a few dollars every game."

By then Napoleon had a job driving a team of horses. Every day except Sunday he delivered wagonloads of coal and wood. His salary was $7.50 a week.

"I could use a few extra dollars," he said quietly. "Sure, I'll play with you."

Nap was a member of the Globe Stars from then on.

One day, when he was about twenty years

old, a stranger came into the stable where Nap was hitching up his team.

"I'm Charles Marston," the man said. "I manage the Fall River team in the New England League. Would you like to play pro ball with my team? For $100 a month?" he added.

Napoleon didn't answer him for a moment. He could scarcely believe he was being offered more than three times his regular salary—and just to play ball!

"Yes, sir," he said finally. "I'd like that."

On May 1, 1896, Nap Lajoie took part in his first professional ball game. He played center field. By mid-season he was batting over .400. Pitchers all over New England had learned to respect his screaming line drives.

One day a scout from the Philadelphia team of the National League turned up at Fall River. He was interested in Phil Geier, the Fall River outfielder. "How much do you want for him?" he asked Marston.

Marston thought Geier was his best player —much better than Lajoie. "Fifteen hundred dollars," he said.

Fifteen hundred dollars was a lot of money to pay for a rookie in those days. As soon as Marston had named that price, he was afraid the scout would turn him down.

"I'll tell you what I'll do," Marston said quickly. "Pay me $1,500 for Geier, and I'll throw in young Lajoie for nothing."

"You've got a deal," the scout said.

So Napoleon didn't even finish his first season with Fall River. He and Geier reported to the Phillies on August 10, 1896. Two days later Napoleon was playing first base in a big-league game.

He didn't break any records that day. He did complete a double play that helped the Phillies beat Washington 9–0. But in five

44

times at bat, he made only one hit and scored one run.

In the thirty-nine games he played for the Phillies that year, however, he made only three errors. He batted a respectable .328. When the season ended, Geier was sent back to a minor-league team. But Napoleon was offered a job for the next year at a salary of $1,800.

"I'll never have to be poor again—if I can just go on being a good ballplayer!" Nap thought. He wrote to his mother that now he could send her extra money every month.

The 1897 season was a good one for Nap. His batting average stayed in the high .300's. In one game against St. Louis, he made a single, a double, and two home runs in five times at bat!

In 1898 Colonel John Rogers, owner of the Phillies, raised Nap to $2,100 a year and shifted him to second base.

Everyone who saw Nap play at second agreed that it was his natural position. He made the most difficult catch seem easy. His throws to first traveled like bullets. Yet he never seemed to strain or hurry to get the ball there on time for a putout.

"He's so graceful!" the women fans always said. And they usually added, "He's so handsome too!"

Other players said, "Nap's playing is as easygoing as he is. He gets along with everyone."

It was true. But it was also true that when Nap left a ball park, he usually left alone. He wanted to keep in good condition, so that he could go on playing well.

That was why he almost never went out with his teammates to celebrate after a victory. Instead, he got a good night's sleep.

In 1899 Colonel Rogers raised Nap's salary to $2,400 a year.

"Now I've reached the top!" Nap thought. He knew that all the major-league team owners had made an agreement. They had said that $2,400 was the highest salary they would pay any player. He was proud to think that now he and several other Phillies earned as much as any ballplayers in the world.

Then he learned that some of his high-paid teammates were also secretly receiving extra money from Colonel Rogers. One of them got as much as $600 a year over his regular salary.

"Why don't I deserve as much as any other man on the team?" Nap asked Colonel Rogers.

Rogers was angry that Nap had found out about the secret payments. "All right," he said. "I'll give you an extra $200 a year."

"But, Colonel—," Nap began.

"Take it or leave it!" Rogers snapped.

Nap realized that he had no choice. The National League was then the only major league in existence. He could go to another national team only if Rogers sold his contract. And he was sure Rogers wasn't going to do that. So if Nap left the Phillies, there would be no place he could go except back to a minor league—or back to delivering wood and coal.

"I'll take it," Nap said. But he wasn't happy.

Then a new major league, the American League, was started. Its owners tried to steal National League players by offering them high salaries.

"Philadelphia is going to have another major team now," a man told Nap one day. "It's the Athletics of the American League. Connie Mack, the manager, sent me to see you. He'll pay you $6,000 a year to play for him."

Connie Mack gave Nap a chance to star in the new American League.

Nap didn't have to think very long about it. "Tell him I accept," he said.

Colonel Rogers was furious. He didn't want to lose one of his most popular players. He started a lawsuit in an effort to get Nap back.

In the meantime Nap was already playing for the Athletics. He had never played better in his life. He finished the 1901 season with the terrific batting average of .422.

50

It won him the title of American League batting champion.

Then the lawsuit ended. The judges in a Pennsylvania state court said Napoleon must play with the Phillies of the National League. If he did not obey the order, he was subject to arrest.

"Don't worry, Nap," Connie Mack, the Athletics manager, said. "We won't let you go back to the Phillies. Our lawyers say you can't be arrested anywhere except here, in the state of Pennsylvania. Of course that means you can't play with the Athletics anymore. But the American League team in Cleveland will buy you. You can play in all its games except the ones in Pennsylvania."

So Nap joined the Cleveland team early in the 1902 season. Of course, he had to take a day off whenever Cleveland played in Pennsylvania. But he did play in eighty-seven games that year. They were enough to show Cleveland fans what he could do. His batting and fielding improved the whole team. The fans loved him.

The next year the National League stopped fighting the new American League. Lawsuits over players came to an end. Nap knew he could go into Pennsylvania without fear of being arrested.

That year he won the American League batting championship for the second time. He won it again in 1904.

In 1905 he became Cleveland's player-manager. The fans had their own name for his team now. They called it the Cleveland Naps. "This year," they said, "Nap and the Naps will win the pennant!"

Every day the fans' dreams seemed closer to coming true. The Naps won game after game. Soon they were leading the league by a wide margin.

Then one day Nap was at his place, at

second base. His team was playing the Boston Red Sox. A Red Sox player slid for the base in a cloud of dust. When the dust settled, Nap was flat on the ground. Blood was pouring from a gash on his leg. The Red Sox player had spiked him.

Nap was rushed to the hospital. His teammates and all his fans were very worried. Every day they waited for the doctors' reports.

The reports grew more and more serious. Nap's wound was not healing. Blood poisoning had set in.

"He may lose his leg," the doctors said.

His teammates were doing their best to play well for Nap. But without him on the field, they didn't have their old speed and flair. Their big lead withered away.

At last came the news everyone had been hoping for. "The wound is beginning to heal," the doctors said. "Nap's leg is saved!"

But it was too late to save the Naps. They finished the season far down in the league.

For the next two seasons Nap worked hard to bring his team back up to its peak performance. He was no longer thinking so much about his own salary. Now he thought more about his players and the fans who came out to cheer them at every game.

Easygoing Nap even let his temper explode if he thought it would help his team. He did so once when the Naps were playing the Detroit Tigers. That day Nap asked the umpire for a new ball. Bringing a new ball into a game was not very common at the time. The umpire shook his head.

"But we can't hit this dead old tomato out of the infield!" Nap burst out. "And it's so dirty we can't see it!"

"The Tigers played with it!" the umpire growled. "You can too!"

He was an Irishman named Tom Connolly,

and he spoke with a heavy Irish brogue. "Get back to the bench!" he ordered.

"Why, you Irish immigrant!" Nap roared.

"You French blockhead!" Connolly roared back. "Get out of here!"

Nap snatched the ball from Connolly's hand and threw it over the grandstand. "There!" he shouted. "Now it's out of the game!"

"And so are you!" Connolly yelled. "Out!"

"Sure, I'll go." Nap grinned as he walked away. "But we get a new ball," he said.

The year 1908 began well for his team. Cleveland was in a fever of excitement. "We're really going to take the pennant this year!" everybody was saying.

By now the fans wanted the championship as much for Nap's sake as their own. "If there's one manager who deserves a pennant, it's our Nap," people often said.

As the season wore on, the Naps were

well ahead of every team except one—the Detroit Tigers. The battle between the two was a close one. Sometimes one team was ahead. Sometimes the other.

The end was a tragedy for the Naps and Cleveland. They lost the pennant to Detroit by half a game!

Nap had put so much energy into managing that his batting average had slipped to .289. Now he made a difficult decision.

"I'm giving up managing," he announced. "I can do more for the team by putting everything I've got into playing ball."

In 1909 he pushed his average back up to .324. His smashing drives made infielders play far back when he came to bat. Then, when he thought the infielder was back far enough, Nap bunted. Time and again he made base hits by placing a bunt that a third baseman had to run a long way to pick up.

In 1910 Nap was competing for the league batting championship with the famous Ty Cobb. An automobile company promised a car to the winner. Both men had their fans, but most of the players themselves were rooting for Nap. They didn't like Cobb. They thought that he would do anything to win.

By the last day of the season, the two men were running neck and neck. That day the Cleveland Naps were playing a double-header against the St. Louis Browns.

"This is the day to wrap it up, Nap!" his teammates said.

Nap hit whistling line drives. Then, when the third baseman had moved far back, he bunted. Six times he bunted, and each time he reached first safely.

That day Napoleon Lajoie made eight hits in eight times at bat!

The fans cheered him until they were

Stars Nap Lajoie (left) and Ty Cobb (below) fought it out for the league batting championship.

hoarse. Those who had been figuring the batting averages cheered loudest of all. They were sure Nap had won the championship.

Then the official figures came out. Nap's final average was .3841. Ty Cobb's was .3848. Nap had lost by seven-thousandths of a point!

The owner of the automobile company said what all the fans were thinking. "Both men are champions," he said and gave a car to each of them.

Afterward the American League officials learned about something that had happened on that last day of play. It was something that might have hurt Nap's good name. They learned that the St. Louis Browns' manager had ordered his third baseman to play far back that day. The Browns' manager, in other words, had helped Nap run up that score of six safe bunts. Even Nap's opponent had wanted him to win the championship!

Fans were surprised that any manager would do such a thing. But they were sure Nap had known nothing about the plan to help him.

"He'd never be mixed up in a trick like that!" they said.

Even Ty Cobb agreed. "Lajoie, it goes without saying," he wrote later, "knew nothing of the scheme. That marvelous hitter . . . didn't need anyone's help to rank right at the top."

The Cleveland Naps never won the pennant while Nap played with them. Nap himself never won another batting championship after those early victories in 1901, 1903, and 1904. But he never lost the admiration of the fans.

In 1912, his tenth year with Cleveland, some of his admirers planned a Nap Lajoie

Star slugger Nap Lajoie began and ended his major-league career with Philadelphia.

Day in the Cleveland ball park. They presented him with a huge horseshoe, for luck. It was made of roses. Hidden among the flowers were 1,009 silver dollars the fans had collected to give him.

Nap's batting average began to slide as he grew older. From .386 in 1912 it fell to .335 the next year when Nap was 38. In 1914 it was only .285. And that year he had trouble with Cleveland's new young manager.

"He tries to tell me how to bat!" Nap told a sportswriter sadly. "Me—who was hitting over .300 when he was still in school!"

The manager let Nap go at the end of that year. Connie Mack, his old friend, hired him immediately. So Nap ended his American League career where it had begun, with the Philadelphia Athletics.

Two years later Nap, now forty-one years old, decided it was time to quit major-league ball. He no longer needed the income. He and his wife could afford a comfortable home in Cleveland and another one in Florida. The poverty of his early days was now far in the past.

But Nap still couldn't stay away from the game. For two more years he managed minor-league teams. Finally, when he was forty-three, he retired for good. He lived for another forty years. He died in February 1959.

In his later years Nap always said that the best day of his life was the day in 1937 when his name was entered in the Hall of Fame. He had gone to Cooperstown for the ceremonies. Fans cheered when he appeared. Many of them could remember watching the easy powerful swing of his bat. Many could remember the way he had streaked for a ball with the swift grace of a cat.

The bronze plaque bearing his name read,

"Great hitter and most graceful and effective second baseman of his era."

"And that's the truth, Nap," more than one man told him that day.

Napoleon Lajoie had earned more than a good living out of baseball. He had earned the respect and admiration of his fellow players, and the love of fans everywhere.

Tris Speaker
The Gray Eagle

Young Tris Speaker had a strong right arm. He never missed a chance to throw with it.

Every night he had to bring the cows back to their barn behind the family house in the little Texas town of Hubbard City. On the way he picked up stones and threw them as far as he could He played baseball with the boys his own age. He always wanted to play with the older boys too.

When he was ten years old, he hung around the field where the high school boys played. "Can I get into the game?" he asked.

"Sure," he was often told. "You can really throw, Tris. You're a good batter too."

Tris's mother sometimes let him visit a ranch near Hubbard City. It was owned by one of his relatives. There, Tris's cowboy friends showed him how to throw a lariat. They also showed him how to ride. Soon he rode so well that he could help break wild broncos.

One day Tris was riding a bronco when the animal suddenly bucked. Tris flew over his head and landed with a thud. The pain in his right arm was so sharp that it brought tears to his eyes.

"The arm is broken, Tris," the doctor said when Tris was taken to see him. "You won't be playing any more baseball this year."

Tris refused to believe him.

"Oh, yes, I will, sir!" he said. "Maybe I can't bat for a while. But I'll learn to throw with my left arm."

68

And he did. Soon his left arm was stronger than his right arm. He went on throwing left-handed even after his broken arm was healed. He began to bat left-handed too.

He was captain of the baseball team in high school. Then he went to college in Fort Worth, about 100 miles from his home. He started to study banking. But the thing he liked best at school was playing on the college baseball team.

Soon he decided that he did not want to be a banker and to sit at a desk all his life. He left college and took a job at a cotton-seed mill back home in Hubbard City. The mill closed down for a few months every summer. That gave Tris plenty of time to play baseball.

His widowed mother was sorry Tris wasn't going to finish college. But she was glad to have Tris at home with her again. She called him her "baby" because he was the youngest of her eight children.

Tris began to pitch for a team from the larger town of Corsicana, not far from Hubbard. "That Speaker kid is good enough to be a professional," many people said.

"I wonder if they're right," Tris thought. He decided to find out.

He wrote letters to managers of some of the professional teams in Texas. He told them he was a good pitcher, and that he was pretty good at bat too. "I'd like a chance to try out for your team," he said.

No one answered his letters.

Then one afternoon a stranger in a horse and buggy stopped to watch the Corsicana team play. He watched Tris pitch his side to victory. Tris also batted two home runs.

"You, boy—the pitcher!" the stranger called when the game ended. "I want to talk to you."

Tris ran over to the man in the buggy.

"I'm Doak Roberts," the stranger said. "I own the Cleburne Club team of the North Texas League."

The Cleburne Club manager was one of the men Tris had written to!

"I'm sure glad to meet you, Mr. Roberts!" Tris said, jumping up on the hub of the buggy wheel. His spikes scratched the fresh

Tris grew up in Texas playing in small-town baseball games like the one shown below.

paint on the hub, but Tris was too excited to notice.

Mr. Roberts looked at the scratches. Then he looked at the tall lean boy with the tanned face. He remembered the way Tris had pitched. "Would you like to try out for my team?" he asked.

"I sure would, Mr. Roberts!" Tris said.

"All right," Roberts said. "Here is a dollar for your train fare. Go to Waco tomorrow and ask at the hotel there for my manager, Ben Shelton. Tell him I sent you."

Tris was at the hotel at 6:30 the next morning. He went to the door of Ben Shelton's room and knocked on it.

"Mr. Shelton!" he called out. "Mr. Roberts sent me to try out for your team!"

"Do you know what time it is?" an angry voice shouted. "Go away! I'll see you downstairs when I get up."

Tris had to wait three hours before

Shelton came down. The man was still angry, but he let Tris go with him to the practice field.

Tris warmed up for half an hour. He pitched for the team's batting practice. He shagged flies.

"I'll let you pitch today," Shelton said to Tris at game time. "Warm up."

"I don't have to warm up," Tris said. "I'm hot now!"

Shelton glared at him as he took up his own position at first base.

Tris did pretty well that day. As the teams went into the ninth inning, Cleburne was winning, 2–1.

Tris hurled the ball. A batter connected and started for first. The runner on first streaked for second. Shelton scooped the ball up from the ground. He tried to tag the batter as he touched base and ran on.

The umpire signaled that the runner was

safe, and the man kept on going. So did the player who had been on first.

Shelton still held the ball. He was sure the umpire had made a mistake. He was keeping the ball as a protest.

Both runners raced across the plate, one right behind the other. The game was over. Cleburne had lost, 3–2.

Tris Speaker told Shelton what he thought of him.

The next morning Roberts was in Waco. Soon he went looking for Tris. "They tell me you insulted my manager," he said.

"All I said was that he was a butter-brained bum for holding that ball instead of throwing it home," Tris said.

Roberts decided the young man had courage as well as skill. He also thought Tris had to learn a few lessons.

"If you will apologize to Mr. Shelton, I'll hire you," he said.

Tris thought about it. "Yes, sir," he said. "I will apologize."

"I'll pay you fifty dollars a month," Roberts said. That was about the usual salary for a minor-league rookie at that time.

Tris made twice as much at the mill. But with the Cleburne team he would be a real professional ballplayer.

"That will be fine, sir," he said.

"For the first month, however," Roberts said, "I'll pay you only forty dollars. I'll use the other ten dollars for painting my buggy. Your spikes scratched it. Your money will have to pay for fixing it."

Tris grinned. "Yes, sir," he said. "That seems fair."

Shelton put Tris on the mound the next day, against Fort Worth. Almost every time Tris pitched a ball, a batter connected. Fort Worth got twenty-two hits. All of them were two baggers or better.

"You're doing fine, kid," Shelton growled at him angrily. "They haven't gotten a single off you yet."

It was a bad beginning for a professional career. But it didn't destroy Tris's faith in himself.

It was still early in the season when a Cleburne fielder was hurt. Shelton had to replace him.

"Try me," Tris said. "I'm a good outfielder."

"Well, you're not much good on the mound," Shelton said. "All right. Let's see what you can do out there."

Tris was eighteen years old that spring day in the year 1906. He was taking his first step toward winning a place in the Hall of Fame. His plaque there calls him "the greatest center fielder of his day." Many experts say he was the best center fielder in the history of baseball.

78

From that day on Tris's name began to pop up in newspaper stories. The stories all said what a fine outfielder he was. They said he was a good hitter too. He helped his team to one victory after another. The Cleburne Club won the North Texas League pennant that year.

At the end of the season, Tris went back home to his mother and his job at the mill. He showed his mother all those newspaper stories.

"Read them, mom," he said. "You'll be proud of me."

She pushed them away. "I'm not interested in baseball, Tris," she said. "I'm just glad to have my baby home again."

That winter Roberts bought the Houston Club and offered Tris a place on it at twice his old salary.

Mrs. Speaker didn't want Tris to be away for the whole summer.

"But it's what I love, mom," Tris said. "I just have to go."

She couldn't hold him. Tris went.

He played well for Houston. In the 1907 season he took part in 118 games for a batting average of .314.

The president of the Boston Red Sox heard about Tris and wanted to buy him. Roberts agreed. The Red Sox sent Tris a contract.

Tris hurried home with it. "Mom!" he said. "The Boston team of the American League is buying me for $750!"

"How can anybody buy you?" Mrs. Speaker demanded. "You're not a slave!"

"You don't understand, mom!" Tris said. "This means I'll be in the big league!" Then he added, "But you have to sign my contract because I'm not of age yet."

"I will not sign any paper that treats you like a slave," Mrs. Speaker said. "Anyway, why should you go all the way to Boston when you have a good home right here?"

Tris had to plead with her for a long time. Finally she put her name on the paper that gave Tris Speaker his big chance.

He spent the last few weeks of that season with the Boston team. But most of the time he was sitting on the bench. During spring training the next year, at Little Rock, Arkansas, the manager took him aside.

Young Tris Speaker loosens up his throwing arm during a workout with the Red Sox.

"The Little Rock team will take one of our players as part of our rent for using their grounds," he said. "So I'm leaving you here, Speaker."

Tris felt his heart sink. He was back in a minor league! And there was nothing he could do about it. "Maybe mom was right," he thought. "Maybe I'm nothing but a slave."

But he knew he couldn't give up baseball.

"I'll show Boston!" he promised himself.

Little Rock won the Southern League pennant that season. Eveyone agreed that Tris was the best player in the league. He led it in hits and runs with a batting average of .350.

Near the end of the year, the Little Rock manager said, "I'm getting some fine offers for you from the big leagues, Tris. Pittsburgh wants you. So does Cincinnati."

Tris tried to feel pleased, but he had

hoped that Boston would want him back again.

Then Boston heard about those offers.

"Speaker is only on loan to you," the Boston manager told the Little Rock manager. "Return him immediately."

Soon Speaker was being cheered as one of the finest players on the Boston team. He was still a powerful batter. But it was his fielding that was making him famous.

He always played closer to second base than any other man in the game. "Why do you play so close?" many people asked him.

Speaker explained. "I have found," he said, "that not more than one in six of the balls driven to the outfield go beyond the outfielder. The rest strike in front of him. I have found it best to be on hand for the short hits and to take a chance on the long ones."

The Red Sox pitcher, Smokey Joe Wood,

once told how Speaker handled a long one. Smokey Joe was Speaker's roommate and friend.

"At the crack of the bat," he said, "he'd be off with his back to the infield. Then he'd turn and glance over his shoulder at the last minute and catch the ball so easy it looked like there was nothing to it, nothing at all. Nobody else was even in the same league with him."

In 1912 Speaker was judged the most valuable player in the American League. His batting average had been .383. He had made 222 hits in 153 games. Nine were home runs. And his fielding had led to many Red Sox victories.

That year Boston romped home with the pennant. Then the team met the New York Giants in the World Series. It was called "the most exciting, nerve-wracking series ever played."

A huge crowd filled the New York Polo Grounds field on the opening day, October 8. When Speaker batted a ball into the stands during practice, more than 35,000 people rose to cheer him.

The Giants got an early two-run lead, but Joe Wood pitched the Sox to a 4–3 victory.

After the game the players and hundreds of their fans left for Boston by special train. The same train carried them back and forth between Boston and New York each evening during the series. It was always jammed. It was always noisy. One group of fans, called the Royal Rooters, sang all the way. The mayor of Boston was among them.

The next day the teams played in Boston's Fenway Park. At the end of nine innings, the score was tied 5–5. In the first half of the tenth inning, the Giants got another run. Then, in the second half, Speaker came to bat.

The Giants' pitcher, the famous Christy Mathewson, sent a sizzler toward the plate. Tris swung and connected. It was a home run! Once more the score was tied. It was still tied at 6–6 when the game was called because of darkness.

Back in New York, the next day, Speaker rode around the field in the new car he had won as the league's most valuable player. As always, his fielding was brilliant. But that day the Giants won, 2–1. The series was tied.

The Giants won the next two games. Boston won the two games after that. Again the series was tied.

The eighth game was played in Boston. In the tenth inning the Giants were ahead, 2–1. Once more the great Mathewson was pitching for them. Speaker came up to bat with two men on base. He popped up a foul fly. The Giants' first baseman started for it.

Then Christy Mathewson shouted to his catcher to make the catch. The first baseman stopped. The ball dropped into the coach's box at first base before the catcher could reach it.

Young Tris Speaker gave a triumphant shout. "There goes your World Series!" he called out to the veteran Mathewson.

Tris was right. He plastered the next ball for a single that drove in the tying run.

Tris Speaker connects with a fast ball for a solid base hit.

Another Boston runner went to third base. On the next play that runner made it home, and the game was over.

The Boston Red Sox had won their World Series. Tris Speaker was the hero of Boston and of the whole nation.

Speaker had also set a new mark for batters to shoot at. He topped the fifty-one doubles Napoleon Lajoie had batted in two years earlier. Tris doubled fifty-three times during the season.

Not long afterward a new baseball league, the Federal League, was being formed. Its owners offered him a high salary if he would leave the Red Sox. Tris told the Red Sox about the offer.

"We'll meet it," the owner said.

So Tris stayed with the Red Sox at a salary of $18,000 a year. He was probably the highest paid ballplayer of that time.

In 1915 the Red Sox won the pennant

again. That time they played Philadelphia in the World Series.

Philadelphia won the first game, 3–1. The following day President Woodrow Wilson watched Speaker help his team to a 2–1 victory. That was the first time an American president had come to a series game. President Wilson threw out the opening ball.

In the third game Speaker's triple gave his team another 2–1 win. The Red Sox also won the next two games and took the series.

Tris Speaker was now more famous than ever. He had a new nickname too. He was given it one day when someone called out "Speaker has spoke!" every time Tris's bat hit the ball. So the fans called him "Spoke."

Sportswriters had another name for him. They called him the "Gray Eagle." His hair was already gray, and he was as swift as a big bird pouncing on its prey. One writer

90

Woodrow Wilson threw out the opening ball at a 1915 World Series game.

said, "He was all 'eagle' in roaming the outfield and making seemingly impossible catches."

Tris Speaker talked in a gruff voice that rumbled like thunder. But his words were always warm and friendly. He was never too busy to visit boys' camps and hospitals for children.

"I don't think Spoke ever had an enemy!" Smokey Joe Wood said.

In 1916 Speaker was twenty-eight years old. The Red Sox owner thought Spoke's best baseball days were over. The new Federal League had failed and could no longer try to win Speaker away from the Sox. So the Sox owner offered Tris a new contract for only $9,000—just half the salary he had been getting.

Speaker refused to sign the contract. The Red Sox traded him to the Cleveland Indians. This was the team that had been known as the Naps a few years earlier when its manager and star was Napoleon Lajoie.

Tris immediately proved what a mistake the Red Sox had made. That year his batting average was .386. He won the American League batting championship from Detroit's great hitter, Ty Cobb.

Cleveland fans rejoiced. They remembered how Nap Lajoie had battled Cobb for that championship. That time Cobb had won by seven-thousandths of one point. "Now the mighty Cobb has fallen," the fans said. "And our Tris toppled him!"

In 1919 Speaker became player-manager of the Indians. He brought in new players. He worked hard with them. Soon they caught some of his own spirit.

They never forgot what he did one day when they were playing the Chicago White Sox. Joe Jackson of the White Sox had driven a tremendous smash to right center. Tris reached it just as it was about to hit the wall.

He struck the wall so hard that he was knocked out. But as he lay unconscious on the ground, the ball was still in his hand. He had saved the game.

In 1920 the Indians captured the pennant. With Speaker they had finally won the victory they had fought for under Nap Lajoie.

Then they went on to beat Brooklyn in the World Series by taking five games out of seven.

After the final winning run, thousands of fans flooded onto the field. "Spoke!" they roared. "Spoke!" Tris Speaker had brought them their first pennant and their first World Series victory.

Tris made his way through the crowd to a little white-haired woman sitting in a box.

"This was what I meant, mom," he said, as he hugged his mother. "This was why I had to play ball."

That day, at last, Mrs. Speaker told reporters she was proud of her son.

Speaker was thirty-nine when he left Cleveland. He was married by then. He had proved he could be a successful businessman between baseball seasons. Even so he didn't leave the game.

He played for a year with the Washington

Southpaw great, Tris
Speaker, gets ready
to run (left) and
moves in for a fly ball
(below).

Senators and a year with the Philadelphia Athletics. He managed the Newark team of the International League for two years. Then he became a baseball broadcaster.

Even at the age of seventy, when his steel business had made him a rich man, Speaker was still a ballplayer at heart. He was looking forward to the next spring training season. He planned to spend it as a batting instructor with Cleveland.

During a visit to his old home in Texas, on December 8, 1958, he died suddenly of a heart attack.

"Texas put him in its Hall of Fame," a newspaper said after his death. "He was as much a part of Cleveland as Lake Erie. Boston called him its own."

The whole world of baseball had loved Tris Speaker, the Gray Eagle. It had loved him almost as much as he had loved the game he played all his life.

THE BASEBALL FIELD

The baseball field is made up of the "diamond," the infield and the outfield.

The diamond is actually a 90-foot square with a base in each corner. This basic plan for the diamond was first written in the rules of the game in 1845.

The bases are white canvas bags, 15 inches square and 3 to 5 inches thick. Home base is a 17-inch square with two of the corners cut off. This five-sided slab of white rubber is level with the ground surface.

The batter stands in a box 4 feet wide and 6 feet long. The pitcher throws from a mound that is 10 inches higher than the level of the base line.

The distance from home base to the nearest outfield fence must be at least 250 feet. The backstop is 60 feet behind the home base. The players' benches must be at least 25 feet from the nearest base line. These benches are in the dugouts.

A Little League diamond is ⅔ the size of the regulation playing field.

right fielder ●

OUTFIELD

● center fielder

OUTFIELD

● left fielder